Melissa

Love you!

Judy

THE
LITTLE WINTER
BOOK OF
GNOMES

THE
LITTLE WINTER
BOOK OF
GNOMES

KIRSTEN SEVIG

THE COUNTRYMAN PRESS
A division of W. W. Norton & Company
Independent Publishers Since 1923

For information about permission to reproduce selections
from this book, write to Permissions, The Countryman Press,
500 Fifth Avenue, New York, NY 10110

For information about special discounts for bulk purchases,
please contact W. W. Norton Special Sales at
specialsales@wwnorton.com or 800-233-4830

Manufacturing by Versa Press
Production manager: Devon Zahn

The Countryman Press
www.countrymanpress.com

A division of W. W. Norton & Company, Inc.
500 Fifth Avenue, New York, NY 10110
www.wwnorton.com

978-1-68268-478-8

10 9 8 7 6 5 4 3

To my husband, Chris,
whom I adore!
There is gnome one
I would rather have
beside me.

A big THANK YOU
to Kari Pearson,
my gnome support
team captain.

Hello, lovelies!

My name is Kirsten Sevig and I am an artist from Minneapolis, Minnesota, who loves watercolor. In order to understand my love of gnomes and how this book came to be, you must first understand that my family is very Norwegian. One could go so far as to say extremely Norwegian. My mother is from Norway, and my father is enthusiastically Norwegian by heritage. The first words they ever exchanged were in Norwegian and my sister and I were raised in the only Norwegian-speaking household on the block.

We grew up listening to the great Nordic folktales, which often featured gnomes, trolls, and other related creatures. The gnome family is quite extensive worldwide, but the gnomes in this book are inspired, first and foremost, by the ones I remember fondly from my childhood.

You might be surprised to learn, as I was, that there is another quite different kind of gnome. I was telling my husband, Chris, an old Norwegian proverb (because of course I was), which led him to ask if there is another word for proverb. I looked it up in a thesaurus and found . . . the word: GNOME! This led me to a dictionary, because I had to confirm this definition and, sure enough, there it was:

gnome /nōm/

noun

noun: **gnome**; plural noun: **gnomes**

1. a legendary dwarfish creature who wears a pointed hat.

2. a wise, pithy saying; maxim.

Norwegian had once again led me back to gnomes, which is how the concept for this book was born. "Wisdom is welcome, wherever it comes from," as the gnome goes, and I couldn't resist this fun pairing, and including a few of my favorite Nordic winter crafts and recipes, too. I hope you enjoy these playful combinations of gnomes—you never know, maybe they will lead you to make surprising and delightful discoveries of your own.

Hjertelig hilsen,

Kirsten ☺

There is no such thing
as bad weather,
only unsuitable clothing.

What goes up
must come down.

We all start as fools...

and become wise
through experience.

Take yourself
lightly.

He who thinks too much
about every step
will stay on one leg
all his life.

Non-Alcoholic Gløgg

Makes 4 servings

This non-alcoholic hot drink recipe is easy to make and ready in very little time. For an alcoholic gløgg, add a full-bodied red wine—and maybe some port or liqueur of your choosing. Consider most of these ingredients optional, too.

Ingredients:

- 1 quart black currant, grape, or berry juice
- 1 apple, cored and sliced
- 2–3 orange slices
- 2 coins fresh ginger
- 2 cinnamon sticks
- 2 tablespoons brown sugar
- 4 cardamom pods
- Dash of nutmeg
- 1 allspice berry
- 1 anise seed
- 4 cloves
- $1/3$ cup raisins
- $1/3$ cup blanched almonds

Instructions:

1. Put everything together in a heavy-bottomed saucepan and warm gradually over low heat until steaming, but not boiling. Simmer longer for fuller flavor.

2. Serve in your favorite mugs or clear jars with a few apple slices, raisins, and almonds on top. Enjoy!

Many a good tune can be played on an old fiddle.

Fortune favors
the brave.

Old love
doesn't rust.

Two balls of yarn
are better than one.

The best things in life
are made by hand.

Snowball Lantern

Makes 1 snowball lantern to be enjoyed outside.

Materials:

· Snow
· 1 candle or tealight
· 1 long match or lighter

Instructions:

1. Make 25 firm baseball-sized snowballs.

2. Place nine snowballs in a circle, touching each other, with a candle or tealight in the middle.

3. Place seven snowballs on top of the first circle, making a slighly smaller circle.

4. Place five snowballs in a smaller circle on top, in the same way the seven snowballs were placed, and then three snowballs in a smaller circle on top of that. Then light the candle.

5. Place the last snowball on top and admire your snowball lantern as it glows! The last snowball may melt and put out the candle, so you may want to wait a while before you put the last snowball on top.

Practice makes perfect.

The way to
a gnome's heart
is through
their stomach.

Cookies are made of
butter and love.

Marzipan

Makes 1½ cups

Ingredients:

- 2 cups (250g) blanched almond flour/almond meal
- 1⅓ cups (200g) powdered sugar
- Approximately 2 tablespoons cold water
- A few drops of almond extract, added to the water (optional)
- Optional additions: cocoa, food coloring, or melted chocolate

Instructions:

1. In a medium bowl, mix the dry ingredients until there are no lumps. (A food processor is really helpful if your dry ingredients are lumpy.)

2. Gradually add water, mixing with a fork and then by hand. Transfer to a clean, hard surface to form a ball of dough. If it is too crumbly, add a bit more water. If it is too sticky, wrap tightly and refrigerate.

3. Form it into balls, logs, or potatoes dusted in cocoa. Add a little food coloring to make pigs, gnomes, fruits, vegetables, and flowers. You can even coat marzipan in melted chocolate to make fancy candies. Have fun!

Imitation is the sincerest
form of flattery.

It always takes gnomes
longer to tell you what they think
than what they know.

The best things
come in small packages.

Only those who wander
find new paths.

Little strokes
fell great oaks.

The apple doesn't fall
far from the tree.

A tree with strong roots
laughs at storms.

Gnomes help those
who give them rice porridge.

Rice Porridge

Makes 4 servings
Active cook time: 15 minutes
Total cook time: 2 hours

Ingredients:

- 1 cup water
- ¾ cup medium-grain rice
- 1 quart whole milk
- 1 teaspoon salt
- 1 tablespoon sugar

Instructions:

1. Preheat the oven to 300°F/150°C and then turn it off.

2. In a medium saucepan over medium heat, bring the water and rice to a boil. Cover and simmer until all the water has been absorbed.

3. Add the milk and bring to a boil while stirring.

4. Once up to a boil, cover and place in the warmed oven for 1½ hours.

5. Return the porridge to the stovetop and reheat while stirring Stir in the salt and sugar.

6. Serve with a pat of butter on top, and sprinkle with cinnamon and sugar. Any leftovers that are not shared with gnomes can be made into a Rice Cream dessert.

A good laugh
prolongs your life.

No one laughs alone for long.

The more the merrier.

Few situations
cannot be improved
by dancing.

It takes two to tango.

A good song
is best shared.

You won't always
know the song.
Sing anyway.

Woven Heart Baskets

*Makes 2 heart baskets
(and wastes less paper
if you cut out patterns for
2 baskets next to each other)*

Materials:

- 2 contrasting sheets of paper
- A ruler or straight edge
- Scissors
- Glue

Instructions:

1. Place your contrasting sheets of paper on top of each other and fold them in half, as shown.

2. Cut a strip at the end for the handle and cut a basket pattern (or two), keeping the folded parts attached.

3. Start to weave the two halves together, inside and outside. This can be tricky at first.

4. When you have woven your heart basket, attach the handle to the inside of each side of the basket with some glue, being careful not to glue the basket closed. Once it has dried, you can hang your basket as a decoration and fill it with sweet treats or candies.

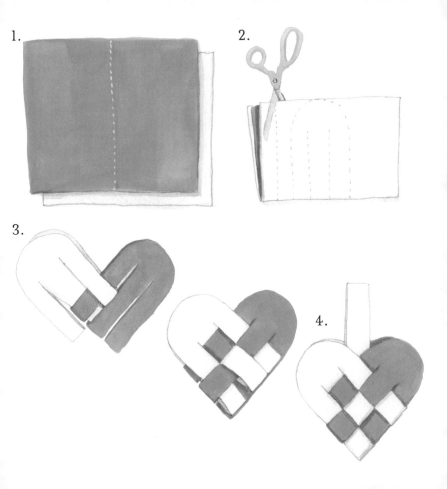

1.

2.

3.

4.

Necessity teaches
the naked woman to spin.

She who chops her own wood
will be warmed by it twice.

Don't start a fire
bigger than
you can put out.

It is better to light a candle
than to curse the darkness.

Rice Cream with Berry Sauce

Makes 4 servings

Sauce Ingredients:

- $1/2$ cup water
- $1/2$ cup sugar
- 2 cups red raspberries or strawberries

Pudding Ingredients:

- $3/4$ cup whipping cream
- 2 tablespoons sugar
- 1 teaspoon vanilla extract
- A few drops of almond extract
- 2 cups cold rice porridge (see Rice Porridge recipe)

Instructions:

1. Heat the water and sugar in a saucepan to create a simple syrup. Allow to cool before blending in the berries to create an even sauce. Chill the sauce in the refrigerator.

2. Whip the whipping cream until just stiff. Then add the sugar and extracts.

3. Fold in the cold rice porridge until evenly incorporated.

4. Spoon into individual serving dishes, and serve with the chilled berry sauce on top.

Food can feed your stomach,
but music feeds your soul.

Many hands make light work.

A warm drink
is a hug in a mug.

Mulled Apple Cider

Makes 4 servings

This is a spiced hot drink recipe, easy to make and ready in very little time. Consider most of these ingredients optional, so adjust to your own taste.

Ingredients:

- 1 quart apple cider or unfiltered apple juice
- 2–3 cinnamon sticks
- 4 whole cloves
- 4 orange slices, or citrus peel and a splash of orange juice
- 2 cardamom pods
- 1 coin fresh ginger
- 1 star anise
- 2 allspice berries
- Additional cinnamon sticks and orange slices, for serving

Instructions:

1. Put everything together in a heavy-bottomed saucepan and warm gradually over low heat until steaming, but not boiling. Simmer longer for fuller flavor.

2. Strain cider into your favorite mugs or into clear jars with a cinnamon stick and an orange slice. Enjoy!

A bird on the hat
is worth two on the wheat.

When the cat is away,
the mice will play.

An accidental fart
should be covered up
by coughing.

It is easier to learn
what you don't need to know.

Keep quiet
and people will think
you are a philosopher.

It is better to give
than to receive.*

* Unless you are a hungry goat.

Don't bite the hand
that feeds you.

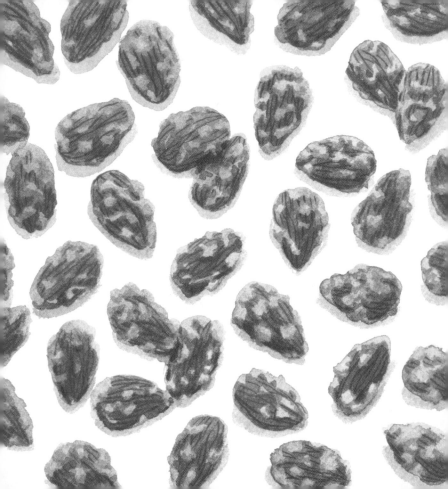

Candied Almonds

Makes 1 cup

Ingredients:

- $1/2$ cup sugar
- 1 teaspoon cinnamon
- $1/4$ cup water
- 1 cup almonds

Instructions:

1. Line a cookie sheet with baking parchment or wax paper, and have two forks handy to separate the almonds.

2. In a heavy-bottomed saucepan or skillet, mix the sugar and cinnamon. Then add the water and bring to a boil over medium heat, stirring continuously.

3. Add the almonds and continue to cook over medium heat while stirring. They'll become shiny and then will look dry. When they turn part shiny and part dry, they're done.

4. Quickly pour the almonds onto the lined cookie sheet, using the two forks to separate and spread them out. Allow to cool. Then enjoy!

Don't waste time looking back.
You aren't going that way.

The courage to continue
is what counts.

Take one step at a time.

Every little bit helps.

The journey is the reward.

All's well
that ends well.

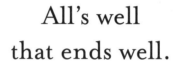